LIFE AND WORK IN OLD CHISWICK

Life and Work

in

Old Chiswick

by

Humphrey Arthure

New Edition

Published in Great Britain by
Old Chiswick Protection Society

Printed in Great Britain by CPI Antony Rowe,
Bumpers Farm, Chippenham, Wiltshire

Author's Note

This handbook was written to celebrate the Silver Jubilee of the Old Chiswick Protection Society in 1982 and to accompany an Exhibition on 'Life and Work in Old Chiswick' at the Gunnersbury Park Museum, in association with the Brentford and Chiswick Local History Society.

Much use has been made of Warwick Draper's history of Chiswick and there has been valuable help and material from many local residents as well as from the staff of Chiswick Library and the Curator and staff of the Gunnersbury Park Museum. Both these institutions have a wealth of information and material on local history.

The instigator and moving spirit of the exhibition has been Rhoda Bickerdike, daughter of Nelson and Edith Dawson, artists and metal workers. She has spent most of her life on Chiswick Mall and Church Street and is herself an artist.

Acknowledgments and grateful thanks are due to J.H. Moya for his fine drawings of houses in Church Street and Chiswick Mall; to James Wisdom and Winifred Heard, Vice-Chairman and Honorary Secretary of the Brentford and Chiswick Local History Society, for their advice and criticism and to Jennifer Stone and Jane Nissen for their help in editing, and finally to my wife, the Honorary Secretary of the Old Chiswick Protection Society, for her constant help and encouragement.

March 1982   **Humphrey Arthure**

Time – like the Thames – moves on, even in a Conservation Area like Old Chiswick. Features such as former wharves are replaced by private dwellings, old buildings need restoration, traffic pressures require to be managed, and meanwhile fresh details and depictions of the area's rich history come to light. In the sixteen years since its publication this small book has achieved wide popularity. This revised and updated edition has been prepared to offer local residents and the growing numbers of visitors who come to enjoy Old Chiswick and its riverside some further background to this delightful corner of London. Thanks are due to the various members of the society who have contributed to its production, and in particular to Carolyn Hammond, Local Studies Librarian at Chiswick Library, for her great help and interest.

May 1998

Alan Munro, Chairman
Old Chiswick Protection Society

Humphrey Arthure's little handbook has been revised and updated several times since he wrote it in 1982. This most recent version has been done by Grania and Alan Munro, the latter a previous chairman of the Old Chiswick Protection Society, and its current president. The Society is very grateful to him for this and for his many contributions to its work.

What Humphrey originally wrote about the attractions of Old Chiswick to its many visitors remains as true today as when he wrote it. Since then a few new buildings have been added to the area and parking restrictions have been introduced. But the atmosphere of a village so close to the centre of London remains. We hope that the information contained in this book will add to the enjoyment of all those who come to this most delightful corner of the city.

June, 2007

Euan Macdonald, Chairman
Old Chiswick Protection Society

Introduction

Whoever thinks a faultless piece to see
Thinks what ne'er was, nor is, nor e'er shall be.

ALEXANDER POPE

Old Chiswick contains many beautiful and historic buildings, among them Hogarth House and nearby Chiswick House and its famous gardens. It is a designated Conservation Area. Many changes have taken place in the last 25 to 50 years, not least the isolation of Old Chiswick caused by the building of the Great West Road and Hogarth roundabout in the 1950's.

Chiswick Mall is one of the delights of London. Any sunny day and most weekends it is fall of strollers, joggers and pushchairs. Thousands come each year to Chiswick Mall, some to admire the old buildings, some to explore the church and its graveyard, while others appreciate the charm of the waterside. Then there is the pleasure of lingering at one of the very few places in London where it is possible to feed Thames ducks, watch heron, geese, cormorants, swans, grebe and even once a stranded seal, paddle barefoot at low tide, launch small boats or listen to a distant cox pacing his crew; in short to enjoy as rural a scene as is possible so close to the centre of a mighty city. In high tide season the road floods – a deterrent to parking.

The village of Old Chiswick dates from early times. Flint and metal implements, together with spear and arrowheads, have been dredged up from the river and several pieces of Roman pottery have been found in the Thames off Chiswick.

As far back as the sixteenth century Chiswick was regarded as a healthy resort to escape to, away from the insanitary conditions in the city, hence its handsome riverside houses. Many fishermen and watermen lived near the river and land was used to grow fruit and vegetables for the London market until comparatively recent times.

The name Chiswick probably derives from the Saxon words for a cheese farm, and although it is many years since any cheese was made here, the name and place are closely linked with printing, brewing and polish making, to name but three of the many industries which have been associated with the area.

The people who live here range from brewery employees to leading industrialists. Artists, sculptors and engravers have lived and worked here and many still do. The artists hold an open day in their studios on one Sunday in late spring and gardens are opened in aid of charity. There is also a fair share of writers and architects. Its inhabitants have a very strong attachment to the area, in fact one of the many surprising things about Old Chiswick is how few people move away and, if they do, how often they return.

This handbook, revised in 2007, tries to give an account of what has happened in Old Chiswick. It starts from Chiswick House in the west and proceeds to Hogarth House and the Reckitt and Colman building at Hogarth roundabout. After Chiswick Square and Boston House on the south side of the roundabout the narrative proceeds down Church Street to St. Nicholas Parish Church and the river, where Thorneycrofts used to make torpedo boats. This is followed by Chiswick Mall, with a short diversion up Chiswick Lane to take in the Griffin Brewery and the Mawson Arms, before returning to the Draw Dock and Chiswick Mall, ending up at Durham Wharf in Hammersmith.

Unloading coal at the Draw Dock, Chiswick Mall

Illustrations

The author wishes to thank all those who have kindly supplied illustrations.

Chiswick House – W. Watts

Life and Work
in
Old Chiswick

Chiswick House, an outstanding example of Palladian architecture, was designed and built between 1725 and 1729 by Richard Boyle, 3rd Earl of Burlington, to house his fine collection of pictures and antiquities and to serve as a sort of drawing room to his nearby Jacobean mansion. It was modelled on the Villa Capra, near Vicenza in Italy, designed by Andrea Palladio in the 16th century. Lord Burlington joined it to his earlier Summer Parlour by a link building. When constructed, the villa did not find universal favour; Lord Hervey dubbed it 'too small to live in and too large to hang on a watch chain'.

3rd Earl of Burlington – J. Richardson

When Lord Burlington died in 1753 his heiress, Lady Charlotte Boyle married Lord Harrington, who became the 4th Duke of Devonshire. The 5th Duke, who married the glamorous Lady Georgiana Spencer, employed John White in 1788 to demolish the old mansion and to enlarge the Villa by adding north and south wings. In the 18th and 19th centuries the house was frequently a centre of political society – Charles James Fox, the Whig statesman and Foreign Secretary, died there in 1806, as did the Whig Prime Minister, George Canning in 1827. Among the visitors were the Tsar of Russia and the King of Prussia. King Edward VII, when Prince of Wales, lived there for a spell with his family. From 1893 it was a private mental home with many distinguished inmates.

The gardens, designed by William Kent, were among the first in England to be laid out in the landscape style, with some of the buildings designed by Lord Burlington himself; from this phase (c 1701–27) date the Ionic Temple and Obelisk. The Bollo Brook was dammed to form a serpentine lake. Many interesting features have been added subsequently such as the Inigo Jones Gateway (brought from Beaufort House, Chelsea in 1736), James Wyatt's Classic Bridge (1774) and the Long Conservatory or

Camellia House (1813). One of the earliest glasshouses in England, the camellias are in bloom in February. The fields between the house and the river are now public sports grounds, known as Duke's Meadows. The Royal Horticultural Society had its gardens at Chiswick House from 1821–1904.

In 1929 the property was bought by the Middlesex County Council, and continued to be used as a mental home. The House is now the responsibility of English Heritage, which has restored the fine rooms and acquired several contemporary paintings and some of the original furniture. The side wings were removed in 1952, restoring the Villa, link building and Summer Parlour as they were in Lord Burlington's time. The grounds are leased by the London Borough of Hounslow for use as a public park. With the support of the Friends of Chiswick House much has been restored to Kent's designs, and his cascade, at one end of the lake, has been rebuilt with help from the National Lottery. The old kitchen gardens are being restored.

Hogarth's House

Hogarth's House is situated on the A4 just west of Hogarth roundabout. The noisy traffic is soon forgotten once the visitor passes through the entrance and finds a delightful old world garden and a charming old house.

William Hogarth, one of Chiswick's most famous residents, took this small country house in 1749 to escape from the noise and smells of London. The window bay in the best parlour looks out onto the garden with its old mulberry tree, which was partially destroyed by lightning in Hogarth's day and by a bomb in World War II, but it still fruits plentifully. The house contains an interesting collection of Hogarth's prints.

Hogarth at his easel – Self portrait

Hogarth portrayed the everyday life of the people, often in satirical vein, and when Garibaldi came to Chiswick in 1864 to see the tomb of the exiled Italian poet of democracy, Ugo Foscolo, he called Hogarth 'il pittore del populo'. Despite being a close neighbour, Hogarth had no time for what he saw as the pretensions and classical tastes of Lord Burlington's circle.

After Hogarth's death in 1765 his wife and her cousin lived on in the house. From 1814 to 1826 it was inhabited by the Rev. Henry Carey, translator of Dante and friend of Charles Lamb. Later the house fell into disrepair, and the studio in the garden in which Hogarth did his engravings collapsed and disappeared. The house was restored in 1891 by Alfred Dawson, the son of Henry, the landscape painter.

In 1902 Colonel Robert Shipway bought the property and gave it to the Middlesex County Council in 1909 for use as a museum, together with 130 Hogarth prints for exhibition. In September 1940 the house was seriously damaged by bombing, but was restored under the direction of John MacGregor, an architect who lived on Chiswick Mall. It was reopened to the public in 1951, and transferred to the London Borough of Hounslow in 1965. It was restored again in 1997 to mark the tercentenary of Hogarth's birth, with a grant from the National Lottery.

The Aegis centre's large office building dominates Hogarth roundabout. The site was previously occupied by **Chiswick Products Ltd.**, which was absorbed into Reckitt and Colman.

Since 1878 two brothers, Dan and Charles Mason, had been running a soap company in Burlington Lane, manufacturing soft soap, furniture polish and metal polish. They foresaw a good trade for boot polish and engaged a chemist to devise a formula. Cherry Blossom boot polish was launched in 1906 and was put on the market at 1d a tin.

Tin of boot polish 1d

This venture was such a success that in 1912 soap production was transferred to Yalding in Kent and the Chiswick Polish Co. was formed with its factory in Burlington Lane, next to a house called **The Cedars,** in which a well known Nottingham

Dan Mason (d. 1928)

landscape painter, Henry Dawson, lived from 1862 until his death in 1878. This house was demolished in 1936 and its site used by Chiswick Products Ltd.

Dan Mason will long be remembered for his beneficent treatment of the staff and workers in his factory. He bought the fine 17th century Boston House in 1922 as a club for the female staff and, with his brother, provided the Recreation ground and Pavilion near the Chertsey Road. He was a great benefactor of Chiswick people, building and providing for the maintenance of Chiswick hospital, which is now under development for housing.

The Chiswick Polish Co. merged with a

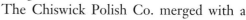

Kennington factory, the Nugget Polish Co. in 1930 to form Chiswick Products Ltd. and this was amalgamated with Reckitt and Colman in 1954.

Hogarth Roundabout is one of the busiest in Britain. When the threat to construct the arterial Great West Road through Old Chiswick was mooted in the 1930's it aroused keen local opposition, backed by Country Life magazine. The scheme finally went ahead in the 1950's, causing the loss of some old shops and houses by the roundabout, an area which had also suffered extensive bomb damage during World War II.

On the south side is possibly the smallest square in London, Chiswick Square, which consists of two houses on each side and historic **Boston House,** all dating back to the 1680's, the latter having been extended and

Chiswick Square and Boston House

refronted in 1740 by Viscount Boston, whose wife, murdered by him for unfaithfulness, has been said to appear. It was sold in 1772 for £960, when it was described as 'the great House and offices situated in Chiswick Square' with a 'great Parlour hung with green Embos'd Paper and Prints compleat'.

Later it became a school for young ladies, after which it was occupied by a Roman Catholic sisterhood, during which time it was called Nazareth House. From 1922 it was used as a club for the female staff of Chiswick Products Ltd. It is currently residential.

Adjoining Chiswick Square is a late 17th century building, now the **George and Devonshire** public house. In 1700 Thomas Mawson, a local brewer, bought the building and two cottages for £70. The curious name of the public house may be a corruption of Georgiana Devonshire, the wife of the 4th Duke, who held social and political court at Chiswick in the late 18th century.

Church Street itself still has a village atmosphere. Until about 25 years ago there was a cafe and a tobacconist's shop opposite the Post Office, run by a well known character, Mrs Byford. Some 17th century pottery was found in her cellar when the building was demolished and replaced by a modern house, No. 6 Burlington Lane.

The old **Post Office and shop** is an early 18th century building with a mid 19th century shop front. In the early 1900's it was a grocer's shop run by Wm. Spencer, but about 1930 Mrs Craig, the postmistress, moved the post office here from the house next to the church and shared it for a time with a barber. It ceased operation in 2001.

Wistaria Cottage is also 18th century and has an interesting irregular roof and a notable porch. Arthur John Sich, a partner in the Lamb brewery, lived here for many years.

On the west side are three charming houses in Page's Yard, leading to the modern **Page's Yard House,** which has a delightful garden. On the Church Street corner of Page's Yard is **Russet House,** covered with creeper. It was built in the 1950's on the site of an artist's studio where Spencer Pryse, artist and lithographer worked until it was damaged by a bomb in World War II.

Ferry House and Brampton House

Ferry House and **Brampton House** were once a single dwelling dating back to the 18th century. In the 19th century it too was owned by the Sich family who ran the Lamb brewery. It was divided into two in the 1950's.

The Lamb Brewery, just behind Church Street, originally the brewhouse of Bedford House, was founded by John Sich in 1773. It stayed in the Sich family until the business was sold to the neighbouring Fuller's Brewery in 1923; the premises were then taken over by the Standard Yeast Co. whose activities caused noxious odours. Since 1950 the building has been used as offices.

Latimer House

On the west side is **The Guardship,** once coach house and then a brewery store. Beer was piped across from the Lamb brewery – the pipes are still there, as is a lift which brought the barrels up from the basement. The name Guardship dates from 1920 when it became a Sea Scouts headquarters. Nelson Dawson, the artist and metal worker, who lived in Staithe House, bought it in 1924 to house his fine collection of sailor-made model ships, and he added a figurehead and ship's wheel.

In the 1940's Mickey Bickerdike made puppets here for an advertising firm. He and his wife, Rhoda, the daughter of Nelson Dawson, used the Guardship as a studio and, until the 1950's, as a marionette theatre, at that time the only one in West London. A special performance was put on after the Boat Race each year for children who lived nearby.

Latimer House might date back to the 16th century, judging from an old oak beam in the basement. It has a fine wrought iron gate and the house was refronted early in the 18th century. Many houses in this area could have been timber framed buildings, later refronted or rebuilt with brick.

In the 1890's Latimer House was owned by James Wright, a builder who worked for the 8th Duke of Devonshire. He divided the house into two and lived in the part he called **Holly House.** He kept a pony and trap in a stable by the house and he used to drive out of Powell's Walk past the church door, which greatly annoyed the vicar. Mr. Wright further annoyed the vicar by building No. 15 Church Street, named October House in 1898, directly opposite the church porch. When the post office moved from here to its present location at the top of Church Street, a florist took over the shop. The house is now a private dwelling.

Powell's Walk is an alley leading from St. Mary's convent in Burlington Lane to the church and it is thought that Powell is a corruption of Paul. The Prebendal Manor of Chiswick and the Manor of Sutton court were the property of St. Paul's Cathedral from before the Norman conquest, and the Dean and Chapter of St. Paul's appoint the vicar of Chiswick.

On the east side of Church Street **Lamb Cottage** juts out onto the pavement. Until 1909 this was a public house, the Lamb Tap, and by it there is a lane leading to offices in the old Lamb brewery building and to part of Fullers Brewery. The Buildings on the right side belonged until 2006 to the E.M. Tool Co. Ltd., which made special purpose machinery.

The Old Burlington and Lamb Cottage

The Old Burlington is a beautiful example of an Elizabethan building. It became a famous inn, the Burlington Arms, and has four front doors, outside one of which can still be seen a cupboard in which drunks were locked up for the night, though some say it was a refuge where patrons could hide from the unwelcome visits of the naval press gang.

It was here that the famous highwayman, Dick Turpin, is supposed to have had his marriage breakfast. On another occasion it is said that Bow Street runners (18th century constables or thief takers) found his horse tied up outside and while they hammered on the door, he jumped through a window onto his horse and rode away.

Some years ago the house was alleged to be haunted – by a man in dark clothes with a black cloak and a wide brimmed hat (he only appeared by day), and by a girl dressed in Kate Greenaway style, with a high waisted skirt and a poke bonnet – but neither ghost has been seen in recent years.

It ceased to be a public house in 1924 and it was extensively modernised by Michael Shepley, the actor, and his wife in the 1950's; they found no less than 25 layers of wallpaper on one wall, including one with a penny-farthing bicycle motif. Earlier owners had found an Elizabethan sixpence under a floorboard. The house has now been divided into two dwellings.

Vine House, attached to the Old Burlington, is late 18th century. The cellar is partly paved with rejected tomb stones (William Nicholls, the builder who lived here was also a monumental mason). Another builder, Mr. Ball, has had his offices in the small courtyard for many years.

St. Denys, now the parish room, has its entrance in a lane leading to the present vicarage. Early this century the cottage contained a soup kitchen and subsequently three sisters of the order of St. Denys lived here and worked in the parish from 1924 to 1974.

The Old Vicarage stands on the corner. A Vestry meeting in 1652 decided that 'the Parsonedge House being so shattered and so very greatly decayed' it should be demolished and a new one built and that this should be 'of brick, very handsome and commodious'. The sum of £260 was collected from the parishioners and after some delay, caused by an extremely severe winter in 1657/8, when the river was frozen up and 'crows feet stuck to their prey', (John Evelyn's diary, 27 January 1658), the Old Vicarage was completed and the vicar installed. The bow window fronting on the Mall

Chiswick, Mddx. S. Woodburn 1807

was added in the 18th century, and **The Chapter House,** in Church Street, was built about 1890 to house the then vicar's large family.

The present **Vicarage** was built in 1973 and the Old Vicarage was sold.

Chiswick Parish Church, dedicated to St. Nicholas, the patron saint of sailors and fishermen, has been for many centuries the centre of life and work in Old Chiswick. The earliest mention of a church in Chiswick is in an Inquisition into the manors and churches of St. Paul's Cathedral in 1181, by which time the Prebendal Manor of 'Chesewic' had been created.

The oldest part of the church is the tower, built by William Bordall, who was vicar between 1416 and 1435. Despite successive rebuilding of the church itself, the tower has undergone comparatively little alteration in over 500 years. Its ragstone walls were restored in 2000. There is now a peal of eight bells and the name of Francis Sich, churchwarden for 33 years, is on the recast tenor of 1869; two trebles of 1901 are named Victoria and Albert. The original five bells date back to 1656, a time during Oliver Cromwell's Commonwealth when such symbols of clericalism were deprecated. The church underwent major alterations in the late 17th, 18th and early 19th centuries, until a complete rebuilding was decided upon.

The foundation stone of the present church was laid in 1882 by Lord Frederick Cavendish. Unfortunately he did not live to see the work completed as he was assassinated in Dublin in the Phoenix Park murders when Irish Secretary under William Gladstone. A window in the chancel was erected to his memory, depicting Christ stilling the tempest.

The rebuilding in the neo-perpendicular style was in the hands of the well known ecclesiastical architect, John Loughborough Pearson, and except for £1000 from the Duke of Devonshire towards rebuilding the chancel, the entire cost was borne by Henry Smith, the brewer, who was a churchwarden for many years.

Mary and Frances, daughters of Oliver Cromwell, are buried in Chiswick but without a memorial. Mary was married to Viscount Fauconberg and they lived at Sutton Court. Chaloner Chute, the eminent lawyer who defended Archbishop Laud and was Speaker of the House of Commons under Richard Cromwell, was buried in the church in 1659, but no trace of his coffin could be found in the vaults when the church was rebuilt. Equally elusive was any trace of William Kent, painter, architect and friend of Lord Burlington, who was buried in the Burlington vault in 1748, in accordance with the request he had made in his will.

It is just possible that the headless remains of Oliver Cromwell are lying in the Fauconberg vault under the chancel. A battered coffin, not mentioned in the Register, was seen by Capt. Dale, son of the then vicar, when the vault was opened but not entered, during the 1882 rebuilding of the church. Great secrecy was observed at the time because the name of Cromwell still aroused violent emotion.

The parish registers date back to 1678 and contain many strange and interesting entries. In 1681 there was a burial of 'Elizabeth Haines, a Nurse Child'. Apparently many Londoners placed children with Chiswick cottagers to be looked after, either because they were unwanted or because it was healthier than in the city; even so, many such children died in epidemics – over 50 are entered in the Burial register between June and December 1781.

Many river fatalities are recorded such as 'Tabitha Davis, who drown'd herself, being distracted', and 'Theophilus Ibbons, accidentally drown'd'. In 1730 Ulysses Lynch 'a stranger, kill'd in a duel' was buried, as was John Elford, executed at Tybourne' in 1749. In 1744 'William Tuck, a supposed Highwayman, who was shott by the Guard of the Exeter coach' was buried, and in 1798 'Thomas William, illegitimate son of Maria Haws and the Soldiers of Kew Barracks' was baptised.

During the 19th century there must have been dramatic changes in Chiswick when streets of small houses were built joining the old village to the High Road. The registers increasingly mention occupations such as bricklayers, joiners, plasterers and glaziers and a corresponding decline in fishermen and watermen. An increasing number of trades are now mentioned, including coal merchants, brass workers, pipe makers and printers – also navigators, better known as navvies, employed for such jobs as road making, but originally labourers on canals.

The Marriage registers show that in the 18th century Chiswick Parish Church was a most fashionable place to get married, many couples coming from other London areas.

Sir Thomas Chalone's monument

Several monuments were preserved when the church was rebuilt, among them a splendid alabaster monument to Sir Thomas Chaloner, who was knighted in 1591 by Henry IV of France. He was a senior official of James I's household and introduced the mining of alum in Yorkshire. His son, another Thomas, became a judge of King Charles I and signed the warrant for his execution.

The churchyard contains many interesting tombs, including a fine classical monument to Hogarth, with touching verses by his friend, the actor David Garrick. Other notable tombs are those of Charles Holland, the Drury Lane actor and Richard Wright, Lord Burlington's builder. The painters P.J. de Loutherberg (d. 1812) and J.M. Whistler (d. 1903) are also buried here, the former in a tomb designed by Sir John Soane, and the latter beneath a fine bronze sarcophagus. In 1827 the poet, Ugo Foscolo, "the Italian Byron", exiled for his support of unification, was buried here. His marble tomb exists, but in 1871 his remains were disinterred and reburied in Florence. There is a handsome tomb of Frederick Hitch V.C., who was awarded the Victoria Cross for heroic action at the battle of Rorke's Drift in the Zulu War. He became a hansom cab driver; his anniversary is still commemorated here by London's cabbies. An 18th century tombstone in the paving by the south wall of the church carries a quaint epitaph in verse: 'Here lies ye clay which th'other day inclosed Sam Savill's soul. But now is free and unconfin'd, she fled and left her clogg behind intomb'd within this hole.'

On 18 June 1978 vandals set fire to vestments and some priceless church music. Great damage was done to the vestry and the organ was destroyed. Funds were raised locally to replace the organ and the work was completed early in 1982. Concerts are held in the church on some summer Sunday afternoons.

A Charity school was built in the churchyard in 1705 and later became a National school. In the account books for 1770 a Mr Charles Hayes supplied 'coal by the chauldron' and materials for clothing. The boys wore blue breeches and holland shirts and the girls wore blue dresses with holland collars and cuffs. The school was demolished in 1951.

There is a fascinating inscription on the churchyard wall in Church Street which records:

> This wall was made at ye charges of
> ye Right Honourable and Truelie
> Pious Lorde Francis Russell Earle of
> Bedford out of true Zeal & Care for
> ye keeping of this Churchyard and ye
> Wardrobe of Godds Saints whose
> bodies lay theirin buryed from vio-
> lateing by Swine & other Prophana-
> tion – So witnesseth William Walker
> V. AD. 1623.

Fisherman's Row (c. 1888)

Fisherman's Place is a modern house, designed by Stefan Buzacs, which, with its garden, has replaced the old cottages in Fisherman's Row or Sluts Hole as it used to be called. Fishermen and their families lived in these tumbledown timber cottages in the 19th century in poverty, but early this century their condition was much improved. A painting by Katherine Parsons in 1905 shows it as a pretty place.

A site for the display of works of contemporary sculpture was established outside Fisherman's Place in 1998 by the Old Chiswick Protection Society, with support from Fuller, Smith and Turner and the Hounslow Borough Council.

Church Wharf was occupied by **Thorneycroft's shipbuilding yards** in the latter part of last century. John Isaac Thorneycroft, the founder of a remarkable shipbuilding industry, built his first steam yacht, the Nautilus, at the age of 17 in his father's studio in Stanhope Street, Kensington. It caused a sensation by keeping up with the University boat race in 1862, and John Thorneycroft started to build boats in Chiswick in 1864. Two years later his father bought up Chesterman's barge building yard which developed into the Church Wharf establishment.

The first torpedo boat built at Chiswick, the Lightning, was accepted by the Royal Navy and designated No. 1 Torpedo boat. Thorneycroft made fast torpedo boats to carry the newly invented Whitehead torpedo. In 1872 John Donaldson became a partner and provided business acumen. By 1885 25 torpedo boats had been built for the Royal Navy with a guaranteed speed of 19 knots, but they also sold torpedo boats to foreign powers, including the Ariete (with a speed of 25 knots) to the Spanish government. This caused some alarm, as a result of which 25 vessels of about the same size and speed, but with a greatly superior gun armament were built for the Royal Navy. These shallow draught boats were also used on rivers in Africa and India.

The Nautilus

About 1879 R.T. Smith, one of Thorneycroft's employees, started a coffee stall in Church Street to try and diminish patronage of the Lamb Tap inn by his fellow workers, and hopefully to save their souls. This was the beginning of the Chiswick Mission, which Smith founded in 1880. John Donaldson naturally encouraged Smith in this enterprise and paid him a salary of £1 per week.

In the early 1890's three '27 knotters' were built at Chiswick, the Ardent, the Boxer and the Bruiser. The last was launched by the four year old daughter of the naval architect, with a lisped invocation of 'Success to H.M.S. Boozer and all who sail in her'. On the 18th May 1893 a 3-funnel torpedo gunboat, H.M.S. Speedy, was launched by Lady Hamilton, wife of the First Lord of the Admiralty. The ship was sunk by a mine in the North Sea in September 1914. The firm also built steam buses, and wagons for the army.

Launch of HMS Speedy, 18th May 1893

As the business expanded more space became essential and the beautiful gardens of the long since demolished Corney House, which stood by the river 100 yards or so beyond Church Wharf, were totally absorbed and built over. Thorneycroft became a public company in 1902 and John Thorneycroft was knighted the following year.

Destroyers were becoming larger and, because of the difficulty of getting them under the London bridges, much of the superstructure had to be added later. It was therefore decided that the Thorneycroft works must be transferred to a site with immediate access to open water, and the move was made to a yard at Woolston near Southampton in June 1904, after which the Chiswick yard was gradually run down.

The closure of the yard at Chiswick came at a time when machinery was undergoing radical changes – steam was giving way to the internal combustion engine. Church Wharf was taken over by **Gwynne's Works,** an engineering firm which made pumps and the Albert car, a model which never became popular. The company switched to aircraft engines during World War I which resulted in local litigation because of the appalling noise and smell during testing.

The original Thorneycroft sheds were destroyed by fire from incendiary bombs during World War II. Apparently two barges laden with wax for Cherry Blossom boot polish were set on fire and burning molten wax spread across the river. Wind then spread the fire towards the church and the vicar rushed over to save the chalices and records. Luckily the wind changed and, except for some lead guttering, the church was saved – all on St. Nicholas's day.

Gwynne's Works left in 1930, after which several firms, including **Lep Transport,** used the sheds along with other marine firms such as The Submerged Log Company, immortalised in the 1960's in a song by Flanders and Swann. Reckitt and Colman took over the wharf and built a massive warehouse, known locally as Lenin's tomb. This also has now been demolished and new houses have been built along the whole length of the river frontage. A lifeboat station has been installed on the new pier.

The original **Corney House** was demolished in 1832. It is possible that the Russell family may have lived in Chiswick in the reign of Henry VIII, but there is no doubt that Sir William Russell, who became Lord Russell of Thornhaugh, lived at Corney House and that he entertained Queen Elizabeth there in October 1602.

His son, Francis, became 4th Earl of Bedford, and it was he who was responsible for building the churchyard wall to keep out pigs. He was a moderate who tried to intercede between King Charles and Parliament, but in the midst of the Parliamentary struggle he died of smallpox in 1641.

After the death of his widow Corney House passed through several hands, including the Earl of Macartney, who became Ambassador to the Emperor of China in 1792, and was the first British Governor of the Cape of Good Hope.

Corney House

Fishing in the Thames. The tidal Thames used to yield some of the finest fish in England. The fishery was under the control of the City of London, whose water bailiff gave an account in 1640 of the fish then found in the river. They included turbot, brill, mullet, sea-trout, salmon, shad, soles, smelt, dace, whitebait, flounders, plaice and eels. The last salmon was taken off Chiswick eyot in 1825.

Last of the eel boats (1898)

In the last century there were in Chiswick more than a dozen eel boats - Peter boats was the old name – handed down from generation to generation, but by the end of the century there was only one eel boat left. Today the river is less polluted and rod anglers are again commonly seen fishing by the Draw dock. The number and variety of fish are increasing.

The Ferry across the Thames at the bottom of Church Street dated back to the late 17th century.

Capt. Dale, R.N., son of the Rev. Lawford Dale (vicar 1857–98) described how, as a child he saw an extraordinary boatload come over from the Surrey side. On one side of the boat sat an old woman with a basket of apples to sell and a couple of workmen with their tools and on the other side sat the Earl of Loudon, the Marquis of Bute, who rented Chiswick House, and the Duke of Norfolk.

The building of the bridges removed the need for the ferry which ceased to function in 1934, one year after Chiswick bridge was opened. The old stone causeway is shortly to be restored.

The Cellars of Chiswick Mall. A walk along the Mall reveals that in spite of the frequent very high tides a number of the houses have cellars extending well below road level. A more careful examination shows that none of the Victorian houses have cellars whereas all the cellars are to be found in Georgian or Regency houses. In fact more that half of the pre-1830 houses either have existing cellars or cellars which have obviously been bricked up. It would appear that high tides at Chiswick prior to 1830 did not reach road level due to the existence of Old London Bridge – demolished in 1828 – which had nineteen wide piers and water mills impeding the flow of the Thames; Old Battersea Bridge with nineteen arches and Old Putney Bridge with fourteen arches also had a contributary effect.

Chiswick Mall has long had a few residential barges, and moored near the slipway where the ferry used to be, are **Leonard Piper, Comus** (now Brevit) and **Mayflower II.**

Woodroffe House is a late 17th century red brick building, with a 19th century bay, named after its 17th century owners. In 1765 a 26 year old girl, Grace Plukenett-Woodroffe married her next door neighbour, a recent widower, the Rev. Arthur Coham, vicar of Chiswick. Together with its neighbouring houses to the east, it formed a part of the Lamb Brewery estate owned by the Sich family in the 19th century, until bought by Fuller's Brewery in 1923.

Early this century Edward Radford, owner of the Standard Yeast Co. which took over the Lamb brewery, lived here and married a daughter of Arthur John Sich. A more recent resident was Wilfred Dudeney, Vice-President of the Royal Society of British Sculptors in 1971.

Bedford House

Bedford House is one of the finest houses in Chiswick Mall. Edward Russell, second son of the 4th Earl of Bedford, constructed it in the mid 17th century in Jacobean style. It was given a Georgian style pediment and fenestration in the 18th century and may have been divided then into the present two dwellings. Edward Russell designed Newhaven harbour and died bankrupt at an early age. After his death in 1665, by a private Act of Parliament, the house was sold to settle his debts.

It was bought by Thomas Plukenett, whose daughter, Grace, born in 1674, married her Woodroffe neighbour and subsequently inherited the whole group of properties up to Chiswick Lane. Her granddaughter, Grace, has been mentioned under Woodroffe House. The first John Sich, founder of the Lamb brewery, lived at Bedford House until his death in 1836, when his son, Henry, took over the house. An elegant gazebo in the Georgian 'gothick' style was built in the garden in the 18th century.

A barrister, Warwick Draper, lived here in the early 1920's, during which time he wrote his history of Chiswick. This appeared in 1923 and was reissued in 1973 (publisher Anne Bingley). In 1928 the house was bought by Sir Arthur Ellis, Physician to the London Hospital. He sold it in 1945 to the actor, Sir Michael Redgrave, who lived here with his family until 1954, when Sir Arthur Ellis bought it back again.

Eynham House

Eynham House was originally part of Bedford House. A 1660 shilling was found in the roof beams in the 1940's. It was also the home of a member of the Sich family. A heart specialist, Dr. Thomas Nelson, and his paediatrician wife lived here in the early part of this century and in the early 1930's he built an extension with a large consulting room on the first floor. During the 1960's Eynham House was the home of Vivian Dakin, a marine engineer, who had been involved with the construction of the old Aswan dam and the Mulberry harbour, used in the Normandy landings in World War II.

Said House

Said House evolved from a small Georgian gardener's house, Said Cottage, in which an artist, Katherine Parsons, lived at the beginning of this century. Sir Nigel Playfair, actor manager and proprietor of the Lyric Theatre Hammersmith, considerably enlarged the building and added the spectacular curved glass bow window in the 1930's. Viscount Davidson, Chairman of the Tory party (1927–30) and later Chancellor of the Duchy of Lancaster, lived at Said House from 1959 with his wife, a member of Parliament who became the first life peeress as Baroness Northchurch of Chiswick. In 2004 it was the home base for contestants in the BBC's 'Apprentice' TV programme.

Sir Nigel Playfair

Lingard House and **Thames View House** were built about 1700. The former was subsequently named after John Lingard (1771–1851), historian and priest. Robert Austin, the engraver and etcher lived at Lingard House from 1930 until his death in 1973. He became President of the Watercolour society in 1956. Among his many engravings were the 1960 pound and ten shilling notes.

Thames View House

Thames View House has the Civic Trust Award 1979 plaque for the flood defence work carried out throughout the Mall by the Greater London Council. Many of the design details of these defences were supplied by the architect, Jeremy Benson of Walpole House, while chairman of the Old Chiswick Protection Society.

Frederick William Tuke lived at Thames View from 1894 onwards. He was the younger brother of Seymour and Charles Tuke, two doctors who ran an asylum for the humane treatment of the insane, first at Manor Farm House in Chiswick Lane and then at Chiswick House from 1893. F.W. Tuke was the Secretary of the Asylum, and he married a Sich. More recently Frederick Mirrielees, an authority on trees, lived here.

Belle Vue and the adjoining cottages belong to the Griffin brewery. Opposite Belle Vue there used to be a mobile crane with which the brewery unloaded material from barges, and later it was used by Chiswick Products to unload wax for boot polish. Then a plague of mosquitoes was traced to bilge water in the barges, and local residents were pleased when in 1955 unloading from barges ceased, because lorries had replaced water transport.

Red Lion House

Red Lion House was built about 1700. For many years it was a public house but it became a private dwelling in 1916. It has a fine staircase and the large sitting room has two fireplaces and a plaster frieze of punch bowls. A large whetstone, now in the Gunnersbury Park Museum, used to hang in the doorway of the Red Lion for osier cutters, who had been working on the eyot, to sharpen their knives.

It was the home of Mr and Mrs Saunders for 1921 to 1941. Their son, Sir Peter Saunders, a theatre impresario, put on The Mouse Trap' at the Whitehall theatre. The architect, John MacGregor, and his family then made it their home for almost a quarter of a century.

Prospect Cottage, only one room wide, belongs to the brewery and is next door to the gabled warehouse.

The Griffin Brewery, owned by Fuller, Smith and Turner, has its main entrance in Chiswick Lane South. Beer has been brewed on this site for over 300 years. In the 1665 Act of Parliament enacted to sell Bedford House to meet the debts of Edward Russell, was mentioned 'two messuages or tenements – being lately converted into a Brewhouse'. The brewery passed into the ownership of Thomas Mawson in 1685. He died in 1714, but the brewery remained in the Mawson family for another 70 years.

The Griffin brewery (circ. 1900)

In 1740 the Mawsons leased the brewery to William Harvest for £180 a year and in 1782 John Thompson and David Roberts from Brentford bought the Brewery from a nephew of Dr Mathias Mawson, the Bishop of Ely.

It became the Griffin brewery in 1816 and a few years later, because of financial difficulties, John Fuller of Neston Park, Wiltshire, was invited to join the firm. In 1845 his son, John Bird Fuller, took on Henry Smith, a partner in the Romford firm of Ind and Smith, and their head brewer, John Turner, forming Fuller, Smith and Turner. The present brewery is still managed by descendants of the three families. The offices are housed in elegant buildings with a fine and aged wistaria, said to be one of the first in England, growing up the facade.

In 1975, Fuller Smith & Turner plc started out on a four phase modernisation of the Brewery. Phase One involved the installation of new equipment to extend the capacity for fermentation.

Phase Two required major changes to the brewery site. A new malt storage

John Bird Fuller

tower and warehouse complex were completed, followed by a fermentation and tank room.

A new copperhouse had to be built within cramped confines, bordered by four existing buildings, one of which was listed. It was officially opened in September 1986 and the new brewhouse was finally completed in 1993. Against this background of change, production capacity has dramatically increased and turnover now exceeds the £100m mark. The Griffin Brewery remains an important and flourishing local industry, with exports going to the USA.

The Mawson Arms

Going further up Chiswick Lane, on the west side are the handsome early 18th century houses of **Mawson's Row,** said to have been built by Dr Mathias Mawson and recently restored. The corner house nearest the Great West Road was originally a private house, but is now a pub called **The Mawson Arms,** and, around the corner, **The Fox and Hounds;** at one time there was also The Fox and Dog on the corner next to the brewery. There was a time when a member of the Fuller family kept a pack of beagles in the brewery with which he hunted in the Harrow area. A blue plaque records that it was in one of the houses in Mawson's Row that Alexander Pope lived with his parents from 1716–19. During this time he published his 'Preface to the Iliad' and 'Eloisa to Abelard', which he may have written in the surviving garden building, now converted to an electricity substation.

Alexander Pope (c. 1715)

~28~

Homefields Recreation Ground was bought by the Chiswick District Council in 1896 and opened in 1902. It was cut in two when the Great West Road (A4) was built and the southern part was saved from destruction by the Old Chiswick Protection Society in 1958, when it was proposed to build two large blocks of flats on it.

There was once a small chapel where the Keeper's cottage now stands, and to the north stood **Bradmore House,** demolished in 1896, where Dr. William Rose, a scholar and close friend of Dr Samuel Johnson, once kept a school. When Jean-Jacques Rousseau had to leave France in 1765 following the publication of 'Emile' he came to Chiswick to be near Dr Rose and lodged with 'an honest grocer', probably in Church Street.

Chiswick Mall and the Draw Dock

The Draw Dock, opposite Chiswick Lane, was very busy in the 19th century bringing in timber and coal, hops and malt for the brewery, and old ships' ropes from the dockyards for the Chiswick Press. The dock was also used by basket makers, using osiers cut from the eyot. In 1997 the railings were replaced in wood, as recorded in Victorian sketches of the scene.

Opposite the Draw Dock is the western extremity of the small island or eyot, covered with osier willows, which is a haven for birds and a landmark in the Boat Race. The osiers were used to make baskets; today local residents "Pollard" the bushes each February. The River still floods into

Osier cutters

the Mall at the Draw Dock when there are high tides, and ducks or swans and even boats may be seen on the Mall. A very high tide occurred in the night of 31 December 1978, before the flood defences were completed, and water seeped into several basements. The danger of exceptional flood tides has receded with the completion of the Thames Barrage at Woolwich.

The flooded Mall

There are two residential barges to the east of the Draw Dock – **Favorite** and **Resourceful.** In 1966 Favorite replaced a previous barge of the same name, which had been the oldest sailing barge by a century and the second oldest vessel afloat. It had carried powder and shot for Nelson. This in turn replaced a splendid yacht, Hermione, twin sister to the first Britannia. In 1974 Resourceful replaced Cetus, a sailing barge built in 1903.

Except at the Draw Dock Chiswick Mall

Sailing Barge 'Favorite'

is separated from the river by well kept river gardens and some fine trees, including oak, silver birch, weeping willows, gingko, almond and Japanese cherry. Most of these gardens were made a century ago, when the riverside was embanked, as early 19th century engravings show open land sloping to the river.

College House (demolished 1875)

The old **Prebendal Manor House** was situated on the east side of Chiswick Lane. Dr. Goodman, Prebendary of St. Paul's Cathedral and Dean of Westminster, was granted a lease in 1562, and the original Norman stone building was then altered or rebuilt for the use of Westminster school in time of plague or other epidemics, after which it became known as **College House.**

By 1684 the old building had become very dilapidated and in 1710 it was replaced by a three-storey brick building. About 1763 it became the home of Agnes and Mary Berry, the 'twin wives' as he called them, of Horace Walpole, and they became his literary executors.

The Chiswick Press was founded by Charles Whittingham. He started with a small wooden press near Fetter Lane in the City in 1789. By 1804 he had begun to use the iron printing press, invented by the 3rd Earl of

A Stanhope press at work (1831)

Stanhope, which is now in the Gunnersbury Park Museum. About 1809 Whittingham came to High House on Chiswick Mall, and in 1816 he moved his presses into College House nearby. He used hemp fibres from old ship's ropes to make fine paper and extracted tar from the ropes, which he used in the manufacture of ink. Many fine books were produced by the Chiswick Press. The business then passed into the hands of another Charles Whit-

Charles Whittingham the elder (1767–1840)

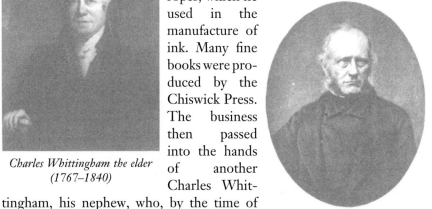

Charles Whittingham the younger (1795–1876)

tingham, his nephew, who, by the time of his death in 1876, was regarded as one of the best printers in Europe. Although a business had been opened in Tooks Court, off Chancery Lane in 1828, work

Chiswick Parish Church, The Old Vicarage, Woodroffe House, Bedford House

continued at Chiswick until 1852. A steam engine was used for making paper, but all the Chiswick Press books were printed by hand power alone.

After 1852 College House was occasionally used as a lecture hall, and in 1875 Ellen Terry played there in a comedy, 'The Little Savage'. College House was demolished in 1875 and all that remains is part of the old Prebendal Manor wall in Netheravon Road South.

Heron House, which used to be called The Hollies, **Staithe House, Suffolk House** and **Thames Bank,** previously Thames Bank Villa, form a group of typical solid Victorian Houses, which were built on the site of College House and its related buildings about 1875.

A row of five elms was planted along the Mall outside College House by Dean Goodman in the 16th century. The only survivor fell victim to Dutch elm disease and had to be felled in 1977. The Borough Council provided a young oak as a replacement, and this was ceremonially planted in May 1977 by Lady Davidson and Ralph Edwards, Patron and President respectively of the Old Chiswick Protection Society.

From 1895 Mr Barnaby, Thorneycroft's chief engineer, lived at **The Hollies** and his son wrote a history of the firm, '100 Years of Specialised Shipbuilding'. Sir Gilbert Flemming, Permanent Secretary to the Ministry of Education, lived here during the 1950's and 60's.

Suffolk House was the home of Ralph Edwards from 1935. He was Keeper of Woodwork at the Victoria and Albert Museum and author of the Dictionary of English Furniture. He was the first chairman of the Old Chiswick Protection Society.

Staithe House, originally called The Yews, was occupied before World War I by relatives of the Thorneycrofts. Nelson Dawson moved here from Swan House in 1916 and subsequently built a studio in the garden.

Thames Bank was built for an architect, George Saunders until the late 1920's. During World War II Pamela and John Newton established an infants school for children who had remained in London. The school later moved to St. Peter's Square in Hammersmith, where it flourished as Thames Bank School for 35 years.

Field House started life as Homefield Lodge, then became Homefield House before acquiring its present name. It was for a time the home of Sir John Thorneycroft's son, who also became Sir John. Between the World

Field House and Longmeadow

Wars it was the home of Nancy Bonner, Baroness of Main. Until recently it was owned by Daley Thompson, the Olympic Decathlon Gold Medallist.

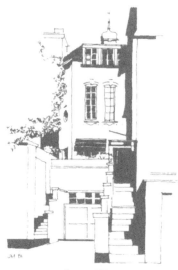

Sutton House

Between Thames Bank and Field House there is a gap, where long ago there were plans to build another bridge over the Thames. This stillborn bridge was to be serviced by a road stretching from Homefields Road across the Recreation ground and into the Mall. Thankfully for the peace of the Mall the only trace of this planners' dream is this open space and the sideways facing front doors of Thames Bank and Field House. A new house with the old name of College House was built behind this square in the 1980's.

Longmeadow, approached by steps under a tunnel of honeysuckle, was built about 1880, and **Sutton House,** or Tree Tops as it was called before 1962, was built in the gap between Longmeadow and Greenash. It has an elegant cupola on its roof, and originally formed the service portion of Greenash.

High House was demolished about 1880 and it is probable that it stood where Greenash now stands. It was described as a jewel of Restoration architecture, and is said to have been built by Sir Stephen Fox about 1700. In 1703 it was occupied by Count Henry de Nassau, Master of Horse to William III, with whom he fought in the Battle of the Boyne. Charles Whittingham came to live here in 1809 before setting up his printing presses in College House.

Greenash, originally called Eyot Villa, is an imposing brick house with an added concrete balcony. It was built in 1882 to the design of John Belcher for John Thorneycroft, the shipbuilder. In 1934 the owner-architect, Ernest Musman, converted the house into two maisonettes and a flat above.

Thamescote and **Magnolia** are three-storey Georgian houses with raised ground floors. Sir Muirhead Bone, official artist to the Admiralty during World War I, lived at Thamescote. In 1918 when food shortages were acute, neighbouring families were invited to fetch hot midday meals from a communal kitchen organised at Magnolia.

Oak Cottage probably dates from the early 19th century and may have been the cottage for the Walpole House coachman.

The Old Chiswick Protection Society successfully opposed the destruction of five houses on the Mall, namely Thamescote, Magnolia, Oak Cottage, Cygnet and Riverside, which the owners wanted to replace with a block of flats in 1957.

Between Oak Cottage and Cygnet House there is a lane which leads to **Eyot Green,** a small group of houses enclosing a green, built in 1960 by the architect, Edward Armitage. Behind Oak Cottage there was a stable, now demolished, which the artist, Victor Pasmore, used as a studio.

Cygnet House and **Riverside** form a pair of early 19th century Regency semi-detached houses with trellis porches. Until the 1960's they were known as 1 and 2 Riverside. No. 1 was for many years the home of Vladimir Polunin, a Russian artist and teacher at the Slade. Although famous for painting the scenery for Diaghilev's Russian ballet, Polunin was better remembered by children along the Mall for the mermaid he painted on his bathroom wall with her tail dipping down into the bath water.

Manning Pike, the inventor, lived at No. 2 and in 1926 he was given the task of hand printing a subscription edition of 'The Seven Pillars of Wisdom'. The house later became the home of a widowed artist, Betty Carver. In 1927 she fell in love with Major (later Field Marshal) Bernard Law Montgomery and they were married in St. Nicholas Parish Church on July 27th. Their happy marriage was ended by her early death in 1937.

Stephen Potter, author of 'Gamesmanship', and his artist wife, Mary, came to live at No. 2 on their marriage in 1939. There was an exhibition of her paintings, including some of the Mall, at the Serpentine Gallery in June 1981.

The Tides

Orford House and **The Tides** (previously called Crostwight) were built by John Belcher about 1887. Orford House was

Orford House, The Tides, Walpole House

named after the Prime Minister, Sir Robert Walpole, who became Lord Orford. It has a half-timbered facade, while The Tides has hanging tiles. CJ.Cornish, author and naturalist, lived at Orford House in the early 1900's. From 1915 to 1927 it was the home of EJ.Maude, later Sir John Maude, who was Permanent Secretary to the Ministry of Health during World War II; he played a considerable part in planning the National Health Service. It was recently the home of Sir Anthony Lousada, a painter who was also President of the Royal College of Art.

Walpole House

Walpole House is a very fine late 16th century building which was altered in the 17th century and refronted about 1730. The wrought iron railings and gate and the imposing porch with its ornamented Corinthian pilasters are particularly noteworthy. Inside there is a fine 17th century staircase said to be the scene of a haunting and a magnificent stone fireplace in the drawing room. The House is listed at Grade 1.

Barbara Villiers, Duchess of Cleveland

Walpole House is said to have been the last home of King Charles' most famous, dominating and amoral mistress, Barbara Villiers, Lady Castlemaine, created Duchess of Cleveland in 1670. She had five children by Charles II, three sons who all became Dukes and two daughters who both married Earls. She must have been a remarkable and beautiful woman, but by the time she retired to Chiswick, two years before her death from smallpox in 1709, she had become old and dropsical. Her funeral took place at the Parish Church, two Dukes and four peers acting as pall-bearers.

The Irish politician, Daniel O'Connell, lodged here for six years, while a law student, when the house was run as a boarding house by a Mrs Rigby between 1785 and 1794. The Hon. Thomas Walpole, nephew of Sir Robert Walpole the Prime Minister, lived here from 1799 until his death in 1803. There is a marble monument to him and his eldest daughter, Catherine Mary, in the Parish Church. Early in the 19th century Walpole House became an academy for young gendemen, run by Mrs Ockerby. The boys marched to church on Sundays wearing mortarboards and Eton jackets. William Thackeray was a reluctant pupil about 1820 before going on to Charterhouse. It is most likely that he had Walpole House in mind when he described Miss Pinkerton's academy in 'Vanity Fair', and where Becky Sharp threw her Dixonary (sic) into the garden to the great astonishment of Miss Jemima.

In 1885 a well know portrait painter, Matthew Ridley, lived here and from 1903 to 1910 Sir Herbert Beerbohm

Sir Herbert Beerbohm Tree

Tree was a tenant. He was a producer and actor-manager at the Haymarket Theatre, and he founded the Royal Academy of Dramatic Art. Dr Shuter of 6 Chiswick Lane described dining at Walpole House one night at the height of the spring tides during Beerbohm Tree's tenancy. In the middle of dinner an agitated maid whispered into Tree's ear that the flood was high in the kitchen and that Cook, who had carried on standing on a soap box, had fallen off and lay groaning in the water. Dr Shuter and Tree went to investigate and found that she had broken her leg, and they carried the cold wet bundle up to her bed.

Walpole House was bought by John Thorneycroft in 1885. He built a workshop in the garden to house his father, Thomas Thorneycroft's monumental sculpture, Boadicea in her Chariot, which was later cast in bronze and set up on the Embankment by Westminster Bridge in 1902 – it is there to this day. Thorneycroft also produced several motor vehicles in this workshop, experimenting with the internal combustion engine, just developed by Daimler and Benz. Later the building was used for dancing classes and gymnastics.

In 1926 Walpole House was bought by Robert Benson, whose wife was a keen gardener and a lover of irises. The Benson family lived in the house for 80 years.

Strawberry House

About 1735 two houses were linked together and refronted by Thomas Peters to form **Strawberry House.** It has a finely proportioned cast iron porch with fluted columns and a balcony covered with wistaria. Beatrice Hindley, who made all the miniature plants and flowers for Queen Mary's dolls' house garden, lived here. Then came Norman Wilkinson, who designed theatre scenery and costumes for Granville Barker's Shakespeare productions. He was also responsible for the present layout of the garden. Frank Bluff lived here after Norman Wilkinson but moved to Orford House after World War II. He owned a large launch in which he often rescued yachtsmen in distress.

Both Walpole House and Strawberry House have beautiful gardens

Morton House certainly dates back to the 17th century and could be even older. The house still has a very old casement window with diamond shaped

Morton House

leaded panes and the original weathered oak frame – this window is on the 2nd floor on the east side, blocked in externally by The Osiers.

A fire insurance plate on the front wall shows a seated Britannia, her shield beside her, holding a spear in her left hand and an Irish harp in her right. This plate was issued to 'Thomas Peters of Chiswick' by the London Assurance Co. and in 1726 the insurance was raised from £350 to £700, a very large sum in those days.

In Queen Elizabeth's reign a compulsory levy had been started for the relief of the poor and for the upkeep of the church – each house was assessed according to its value and size. In 1726 the rate for Thomas Peters' house jumped from £11 to £20 but did not change for neighbouring houses. Because of its sudden increase in value it seems likely that Thomas Peters had recently faced the old timber framed house with the brick facade we still see. About 1958 the brickwork of the front of the house began to bulge outwards, probably the end result of a local flying bomb in World War II. The facade was then rebuilt – each brick in its original place, except for those which had disintegrated and these were replaced with exact copies, stitched into place with thick copper wire and cemented.

Morton House has had many distinguished residents over the centuries. From about 1923 it housed a famous artist and sculptor, Eric Kennington, whose studio was in Durham Wharf at the east end of Chiswick Mall. One of his works was the 24th Division War Memorial in Battersea Park. He also sculpted a figure of his friend, TE. Lawrence (Lawrence of Arabia), for his tomb, and he illustrated 'The Seven Pillars of Wisdom'. From 1937 Sir Percy Harris, Chief Whip for the Liberal Party (1935–45) lived here; he was a strong supporter of the League of Nations.

Dr. Maurice Shaw, Physician to the West London Hospital, lived at Morton House from 1953 until his death in 1977. He was chairman of the Brentford and Chiswick Local History Society for 13 years. His wife, Christine, did meticulous research into local history and was a member of the History Society from its beginning in 1958. A small part of her research into the history of Morton House is published here. Christine Shaw was also the first Honorary Secretary of the Old Chiswick Protection Society.

The Osiers was built about 1786 and was refaced with stucco early in the 19th century. Leonard Colebrook, Pathologist to Queen Charlotte's Maternity Hospital, lived here before and during World War II; he played an important part in overcoming the dangers of puerperal fever, until then the greatest scourge of childbirth.

Chiswick Lodge was built in 1912 by Dan Mason as a cottage hospital for the people of Chiswick. It was built on the site of **Rothbury House,** the home of Admiral Sir Robert Smart from 1850 to 1875 and of George Chibnall, owner of the bakery further along the Mall, in this century. Although it ceased to function as a maternity hospital in 1974 it was reopened as Chiswick Lodge to care for the elderly infirm. The site is being developed for housing.

Island House

St. Johns, Norfolk House and **Island House,** previously called Waltham Lodge, form a group of early 19th century stucco houses. Island House has Corinthian pilasters. Arthur Sich lived here in the 1880's and Norfolk House was the home of the Sich family for many years. Perhaps the most notable occupant was Alexander Sich, who was most active in municipal government and was described as one of the keenest hearted men that ever lived; he died in 1916.

John Sich the second (1781–1855). Eldest son of John Sich who founded the Lamb brewery. He was a Lieutenant in the Corps of Chiswick Volunteers formed when Napoleon threatened invasion.

Swan House and **Cedar House** were built in the late 17th century. **Swan House** has many artistic and literary associations. Nelson Dawson married an artist, Edith Robinson, in 1893 and they worked in hand-wrought metals and enamelling, becoming world famous. Nelson Dawson was also a water colour artist and etcher and he illustrated E.V Lucas's 'Highways and Byways of London'. Their daughter, Rhoda, was an accomplished artist in woodcut. A quaker, she was one of Chiswick's great characters and died in 1992. Sir John Squire, author, poet and editor of the London Mercury, was a tenant from 1916 to 1925. He was followed

Swan House

Nelson and Edith Dawson with their two daughters (circ. 1908)

by Sir George Rostrevor Hamilton who edited 'Poems of Today' and wrote 'Rapids of Time', as well as being a collector of butterflies.

Cedar House, once called The Malt House, has large bow windows facing east. It was used as offices by Chibnall's bakery (which became Miller's bakery), but is now once again an attractive private dwelling.

There is a stone inscribed 'H'mth' by the entrance to Cedar House, marking what used to be the boundary between Chiswick and Hammersmith. This is today the boundary of the London Borough of Hounslow.

The neo-Georgian houses at **Miller's Court,** designed by architects Chapman and Taylor, are so named because the houses were built on the site of **Miller's bakery.** Sacks of flour were unloaded at the wharf opposite and brought across the Mall to be hoisted to the upper floor of the bakery. Baking ceased in 1966 and the buildings were demolished in 1969.

UNDER IDEAL CONDITIONS
ON THE BANK OF THE THAMES

THE MILL BAKERIES – THE MALL W.4.

Miller's bakery (demolished 1969)

Opposite Miller's Court there used to be a creek, now filled in, and the hump in the road probably marks a minor branch of Stamford Brook.

Slightly further on, on the river side of the Mall, there is a group of houses – Eyot Cottage, which was two cottages (Ait and Willow) joined together, **Mall Cottage,** originally Gothic Cottage, and **The Willows.**

From 1900 to the 1930's Eyot Cottage housed an architect and furniture designer, Charles Spooner and his wife, Minnie, a children's portraitist and illustrator of children's books. More recently it was the home of a naval engineer, James Ritchie, whose wife was the daughter of Warwick Draper, the Chiswick historian. Ernest Jackson, who taught drawing at the Royal Academy School of Art, used to live in Mall Cottage. He designed posters for the London Underground from 1913 for some years.

The Sculptor Eric Kennington used part of **Durham Wharf,** just beyond The Willows, as his studio. A.P. Herbert, later Sir Alan, who lived in Hammersmith Terrace, and Eric Kennington owned a small canal houseboat, moored off Durham Wharf, in which a New Zealander, Len Lye, created hand painted abstract films, which became popular in the 1930's.

Joyce Clissold also worked at Durham Wharf in the 1920's and employed many local girls in her textile design business, Footprints. She still continues to design textiles at The Butts, Brentford. When Miss Clissold left there was a baker's shop at Durham Wharf and later a greengrocer's. For the last 45 years it has been the studio of well known artists, Mary Fedden and the late Julian Trevelyan. They also built the adjacent studio dwellings in the 1970's for artists to live and work in.

Durham Wharf brings us to the end of Chiswick Mall, and so to the end of this short account of life and work in Old Chiswick.